Little Pebble™

Transport

# Lorries

by Mari Schuh

raintree
a Capstone company — publishers for children

Raintree is an imprint of Capstone Global Library Limited, a company incorporated in England and Wales having its registered office at 264 Banbury Road, Oxford, OX2 7DY – Registered company number: 6695582

**www.raintree.co.uk**
myorders@raintree.co.uk

Edited by Carrie Braulick Sheely
Designed by Lori Bye
Picture research by Wanda Winch
Production by Laura Manthe
Originated by Capstone Global Library Limited
Printed and bound in China

ISBN 978 1 4747 4429 4
21 20 19 18 17
10 9 8 7 6 5 4 3 2 1

**British Library Cataloguing in Publication Data**
A full catalogue record for this book is available from the British Libra

**Acknowledgements**
We would like to thank the following for permission to reproduce phot      raphs: Alamy Stock Photo:      outh
West Images Scotland, 7, Transport/Stephen Barnes, 8–9; Capstone Stu        o: Karon Dubke; H. Dream      ime:
Davidebner, 21; iStockphoto: 8c061bbf_466, 12–13; Shutterstock: Adrian Reynolds, cover, Kisan, steel design,
Mario Pantelic, lines design, Mike Brake, 17, Paul J. Martin, 5, Robert J. Beyers II, 15, T. Sumaetho, zoom
motion design, Tony Baggett, 19

# Contents

# On the road

What's that noise?

A big lorry goes down the road.

Here it comes!

Lorries haul loads.

They can carry logs.

See them go!

# Parts

Lorries have big engines.

They often use diesel fuel.

The cab is at the front.

The driver sits in the cab.

She starts the engine.

Let's go!

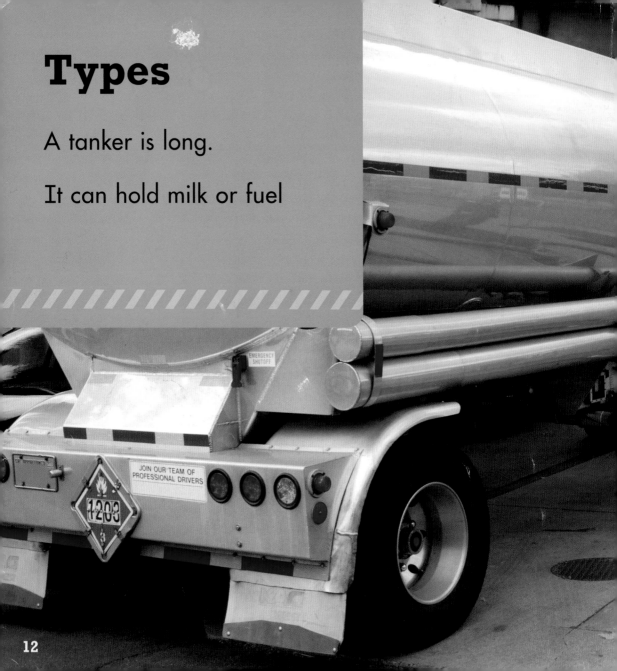

# Types

A tanker is long.

It can hold milk or fuel

13

A dumper truck has a bed.

The bed holds heavy loads.

It tips up.

It dumps the load!

A fire engine puts out fires.

It has long hoses.

Whoosh!

They spray water.

A bin lorry is busy.

It picks up lots of rubbish.

It goes to the landfill.

Monster trucks have big wheels.

These trucks fly through the air.

They smash cars flat!

# Glossary

**bed**   back end of a dumper truck; the bed tips up to dump loads

**cab**   area for a driver to sit in a large truck or machine

**diesel fuel**   heavy fuel that burns to make power

**engine**   machine in which fuel burns to provide power

**haul**   pull or carry a load

**landfill**   place where rubbish is buried

**load**   anything that must be lifted and carried by a vehicle, person or machine

# Find out more

## Books

*Big Machines Drive!* (Big Machines), Catherine Veitch (Raintree, 2015)

*Look Inside Things That Go* (Usborne Look Inside) Rob Lloyd Jones (Usborne Publishing Ltd, 2013)

*Machines on the Road* (Machines at Work), Sian Smith (Raintree, 2014)

*Trucks* (Usborne Beginners), Katie Daynes (Usborne Publishing Ltd, 2007)

## Websites

www.dkfindout.com/uk/search/transport/
Learn about different types of transport.

http://www.bbc.co.uk/education/clips/zj3myrd
Discover the type of fuel that lorries use.

# Comprehension questions

1. Name two parts that trucks often have in common.

2. Why might people use trucks instead of other vehicles?

3. Name two ways that trucks can help people.

# Index